CW01305351

FACE READING ESSENTIALS

MOUTH

Connection

Desire

Expression

JOEY YAP

Face Reading Essentials - MOUTH

Copyright © 2009 by Joey Yap
All rights reserved worldwide.
First Edition June 2009

All intellectual property rights contained or in relation to this book belongs to Joey Yap.

No part of this book may be copied, used, subsumed, or exploited in fact, field of thought or general idea, by any other authors or persons, or be stored in a retrieval system, transmitted or reproduced in any way, including but not limited to digital copying and printing in any form whatsoever worldwide without the prior agreement and written permission of the author.

The author can be reached at:

Mastery Academy of Chinese Metaphysics Sdn. Bhd. (611143-A)
19-3, The Boulevard, Mid Valley City,
59200 Kuala Lumpur, Malaysia.
Tel   : +603-2284 8080
Fax   : +603-2284 1218
Website : www.masteryacademy.com

DISCLAIMER:

The author, Joey Yap and the publisher, JY Books Sdn Bhd, have made their best efforts to produce this high quality, informative and helpful book. They have verified the technical accuracy of the information and contents of this book. Any information pertaining to the events, occurrences, dates and other details relating to the person or persons, dead or alive, and to the companies have been verified to the best of their abilities based on information obtained or extracted from various websites, newspaper clippings and other public media. However, they make no representation or warranties of any kind with regard to the contents of this book and accept no liability of any kind for any losses or damages caused or alleged to be caused directly or indirectly from using the information contained herein.

Published by JY Books Sdn. Bhd. (659134-T)

INDEX

	Introduction	iv
	Basic Mouth Shapes	15
1	One-Character Mouth	16
2	Four-Character Mouth	18
3	Square Mouth	20
4	Wide Mouth	22
5	Thin Cut Mouth	24
6	Crooked Mouth	26
7	Flagged Mouth	28
8	Smiling Mouth	30
9	Wrinkled Mouth	32
10	Wavering Mouth	34
11	Lower Reserved Mouth	36
12	The Revealing Mouth	38
13	Unrevealed Teeth Mouth	40
14	The Drooling Mouth	42
15	Upper Lip Biting Lower Lip	44
16	Lower Lip Biting Upper Lip	46
17	Lines on Lower Lips	48
18	Unbalanced Lips	50
19	Protruding Lips	52

口
相

20	Sunken Lips	54
21	Solitary Life Lines	56
	Unique Mouth Shapes	59
22	Blowing Fire Mouth	60
23	Cherry Mouth	62
24	Lotus Leaf Mouth	64
25	Grained Mouth	66
26	Satchel Mouth	68
27	Crescent Moon Mouth	70
28	Bow-Shaped Mouth	72
29	The Curved Bow Crescent Moon Mouth	74
30	Swoosh Shape Mouth	76
31	Sword Handle Mouth	78
32	Ocean Mouth	80
33	Reverse Boat Mouth	82
34	Pearl in the Sea Mouth	84
35	Island in the Sea Mouth	86
	Animal Shape Mouths	89
36	Monkey Mouth	90
37	Snake Mouth	92
38	Cow Mouth	94
39	Pigeon Mouth	96

40	Dragon Mouth	98
41	Horse Mouth	100
42	Carp Mouth	102
43	Fish Head Mouth	104
44	Bird Beak Mouth	106
45	Rat Mouth	108
46	Tiger Mouth	110
47	Goat Mouth	112
48	Pig Mouth	114

MASTERY ACADEMY
OF CHINESE METAPHYSICS™

At **www.masteryacademy.com**, you will find some useful tools to ascertain key information about the Feng Shui of a property or for the study of Astrology.

The Joey Yap Flying Stars Calculator can be utilised to plot your home or office Flying Stars chart. To find out your personal best directions, use the 8 Mansions Calculator. To learn more about your personal Destiny, you can use the Joey Yap BaZi Ming Pan Calculator to plot your Four Pillars of Destiny – you just need to have your date of birth (day, month, year) and time of birth.

For more information about BaZi, Xuan Kong or Flying Star Feng Shui, or if you wish to learn more about these subjects with Joey Yap, logon to the Mastery Academy of Chinese Metaphysics website at **www.masteryacademy.com**.

MASTERY ACADEMY
E-LEARNING CENTER

www.maelearning.com

Bookmark this address on your computer, and visit this newly-launched website today. With the E-Learning Center, knowledge of Chinese Metaphysics is a mere 'click' away!

Our E-Learning Center consists of 3 distinct components.

1. Online Courses
These shall comprise of 3 Programs: our Online Feng Shui Program, Online BaZi Program, and Online Mian Xiang Program. Each lesson contains a video lecture, slide presentation and downloadable course notes.

2. MA Live!
With MA Live!, Joey Yap's workshops, tutorials, courses and seminars on various Chinese Metaphysics subjects broadcasted right to your computer screen. Better still, participants will not only get to see and hear Joey talk 'live', but also get to engage themselves directly in the event and more importantly, TALK to Joey via the MA Live! interface. All the benefits of a live class, minus the hassle of actually having to attend one!

3. Video-On-Demand (VOD)
Get immediate streaming-downloads of the Mastery Academy's wide range of educational DVDs, right on your computer screen. No more shipping costs and waiting time to be incurred!

Study at your own pace, and interact with your Instructor and fellow students worldwide…at your own convenience and privacy. With our E-Learning Center, knowledge of Chinese Metaphysics is brought DIRECTLY to you in all its clarity, with illustrated presentations and comprehensive notes expediting your learning curve!

Welcome to the Mastery Academy's E-LEARNING CENTER…
YOUR virtual gateway to Chinese Metaphysics mastery!

INTRODUCTION : THE BASICS OF Face Reading

The idea for the Face Reading Essentials series of books began out of my wish to simplify what is a sophisticated, multifaceted study into something a little easier to digest. Chinese Face Reading has a long and illustrious history, and was first developed around the time of the Yellow Emperor, Huang Di (2700 BC – 2150 BC). It was used extensively by royal advisors and strategists throughout the Imperial Dynasty. It was also a large part of traditional Chinese culture, where mothers-in-law would vet their children's potential spouses by applying a spot of savvy Face Reading during initial meetings!

The art and practice of Face Reading, or Mian Xiang as it's known in Chinese (and I'll be using the terms 'Face Reading' and 'Mian Xiang' interchangeably) is one that is comprised of various elements and composites. There is a lot of information to process – face shape, individual features and its respective traits, facial expressions, Qi colours, and so on – and for the general beginner, this can be overwhelming and daunting.

These days, we're all pressed for time and don't have the resources to go through a "getting to know you" stage before deciding whether or not we like someone or find them suitable – whether it is a job interview, first date, or a business negotiation. Deciding to pick the 'right' someone can be fraught with tension and anxiety. Face Reading can be the ideal time-saving tool that can help you make quick decisions that are effective and accurate.

Mian Xiang uses two primary techniques to read a face: Fixed Position Reading, and Combination Position Reading. A Fixed Position Reading simply looks at a specific point or feature in the face to gain insight to a particular subject in question, while Combination Position Reading will give you a more in-depth, detailed analysis of a particular subject, taking into account several factors and not just one area or feature of the face. The Face Reading Essentials books teach you how to do a Fixed Position Reading, which is the ideal starting point for beginners, being as it is simple and easy to learn but no less effective.

With these books, you get the most relevant and user-friendly information broken-down into sizeable portions and bite-sized chunks. By user-friendly, I mean that you can just point to one of the detailed illustrations of a feature, read the short accompanying description, and be able to point it out on your face, or on the faces of the people around you!

The Mouth Speaks Volumes

"He was so attractive until he opened his mouth and spoke." How many times have we heard something like that?

The mouth is the primary way by which we get to know what someone is thinking. People give expression to their thoughts and feelings by uttering them aloud. There is a Chinese saying that goes, "A filthy mouth will not utter decent language." In Mian Xiang, however, the mouth can tell you more about the person than the words they choose to say. You can observe the qualities and traits of the mouth to learn more about the subtle, unrevealed information about a person's communication skills and their essential, basic natures.

A key aspect in Mian Xiang study and practice is the concept of the 5 Officers, where each of the 5 Officers correspond to five main features of the face – the eyes, eyebrows, ears, nose, and mouth. The mouth is known as the Communications Officer. It will tell you how you communicate with others as well as revealing the quality of that communication – which in turn determines the quality of your relationships and connections, and the quality of your life in general.

The shape and formation of your mouth can reveal if you have the ability to sway and persuade others to your opinion, and whether your communication has power, grace, and effectiveness. It can also divulge information about a person's basic character – whether they're warm and generous, emotional and sincere, or mean-

口相

spirited, cold, and manipulative. The thickness of the lips, for example, can reflect a person's attitude towards relationships and romantic connections. Want to know if someone will be benevolent and giving, or selfish and self-serving? Look at the mouth!

In addition, in Mian Xiang, the mouth is indicative of how we'll fare in our latter years – whether it'll be a happy life surrounded by loved ones, or a lonely, isolated one riddled with hardships.

Each and Every Mouth is Unique

The information in this book is a culmination of many years of research into various methods, techniques and interpretations given in the classical texts of Mian Xiang. I've put it together here in a way that I hope facilitates immediate use of the information, and in a manner that I also hope is simple and easily-understandable!

It's important to remember that no particular mouth is ever just one type of mouth. Most of us have mouths that are a combination of factors and attributes, which is why people are a lot more complex than we care to imagine! For example, your mouth could be a combination of a Wide Mouth with Unbalanced Lips, or Protruding Lips with a Revealing Mouth. You will find this to be true for most everyone you know, which is why Face Reading requires you to be able to synthesise the information presented instead of thinking in 'either/or' and 'black-and-white' terms.

This is the reason why I emphasise that the two most important tools in Face Reading are a mirror and an open mind! Holding up a mirror as you read the book will help you physically imagine these features and types. But equally important is to rid yourself of the notion of a "fixed" type or quality, because the practice of Face Reading should be fluid, contextual, and discerning. The information presented here is categorised into types so that it's easier to learn and be understood, but people don't come in fixed types or categories – so Face Reading is all about putting the information together in creative ways, bearing in mind the context it is in, in order to obtain the bigger picture.

Should you wish to learn more about the intricacies of Mian Xiang study and practice, you might want to consider my online Face Reading classes via the Mastery Academy E-Learning Centre (www.maelearning.com). My other book, *Mian Xiang – Discover Face Reading* is a detailed, solid introduction to Mian Xiang, and can also serve as a great reference accompaniment to the Face Reading Essentials books. You might also want to try *Joey Yap's Art of Face Reading*, which puts a more thorough spin on Face Reading and shows you how to put together information about individual features and traits to read faces (Combination Face Reading).

But what I wish to stress with this book is that Face Reading is, and should be, fun! Being handy and pocket-sized, you can whip it out at any point in time (it would make a great conversation-starter in parties and gatherings) and go through it with friends and family. It's designed to be easy – simply point, and refer. And always remember that while you should never judge a book by its cover, the face has many stories to tell... and it rarely ever lies!

Here's to many hours of pleasure and discovery with this book in hand.

Joey Yap
June 2009

Author's personal websites :
www.joeyyap.com | www.fengshuilogy.com (Personal blog)

Academy websites :
www.masteryacademy.com | www.masteryjournal.com |
www.maelearning.com

Follow Joey's current updates on Twitter :
www.twitter.com/joeyyap

Basic Mouth Shapes

One-Character Mouth 一字口

The one-character mouth refers to a flat mouth, and gets its name from the "one character' in the Chinese language. People with this mouth have modest, self-contained personalities. They're always known as being 'the responsible ones!'

Typically, they don't place much value on money or a materialistic life. They refrain from making comments about anyone or anything, and are very committed to living a balanced and wholesome lifestyle.

"Everything in moderation" is their battle cry, and with an aim for a life of middling complacency, they don't always hit the mark for outstanding achievement. They're serious about their work, but lack the fire and ambition to excel or be the best.

口相

Four-Character Mouth 四字口

The Four-Character Mouth is square-like in appearance, with both the upper and lower lips being of similar thickness and width. The mouth is usually a vibrant red colour.

People with Four-Character Mouths are strong on sentiment, and empathetic towards others. They are fiercely loyal to those whom they care about. They frequently excel in examinations, and are very public service-oriented, always being involved in lots of community and voluntary work.

Because of their good-natured spirit and their inclination to help others, they will enjoy success in many phases of their life. These are the kind of people who are most likely to lead long, happy, and productive lives.

口相

19

Square Mouth 方口

A Square Mouth is generally not a very large mouth, but it does have an obvious cubic or square-like appearance. People with this type of mouth will find it easy to reach the upper echelons of society without much effort at all.

They usually have a very practical and pragmatic approach to life, and are diplomatic and tactful, winning them much regard from others. They are confident and capable, and others always find them dependable and reliable.

These are not the kind of people who can usually found scrambling about at the last minute, putting their helter-skelter pieces of life back together! Being systematic and organised is part of their inherent nature.

口相

21

Wide Mouth 闊大口

When we speak of Wide Mouths, we're referring to a wide mouth that is characterised by thick, generous lips. People with Wide Mouths usually have benevolent, magnanimous natures.

They possess strong leadership skills, and are very influential. They are energetic and are very outgoing and gregarious, and possess high hopes and dreams that correspond to their ideals.

They have the passion and the motivation to go after their dreams, and they like to be in control. It works out for well for them, because they are often able to steer their ship according to their drives and ambitions. As a result of this, more often than not, they are able to achieve their goals.

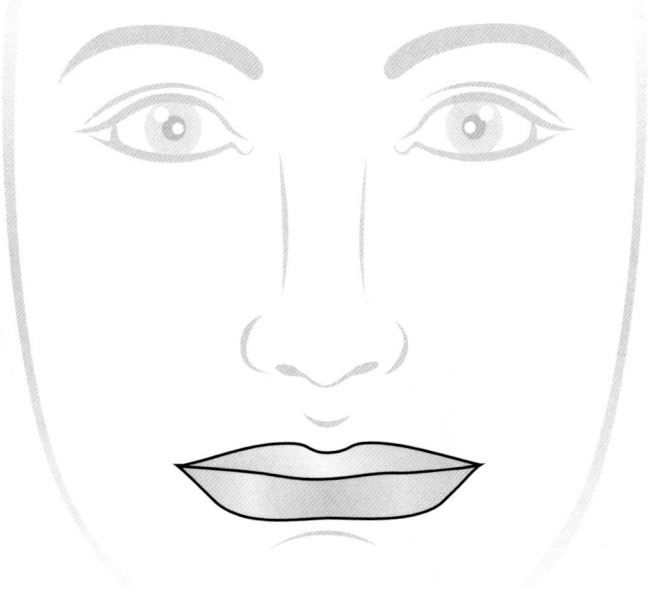

口相

23

Thin Cut Mouth 薄削口

A Thin Cut Mouth is when both the upper and lower lips are thin, and the corners are sharp and pointy. The most defining characteristic of a person with a Thin Cut Mouth? His or her words are as sharp as the corners of their mouth!

The more they say, the more they're likely to get into trouble. And despite being clever, Thin Cut Mouth people will always like shortcuts and the easy, fast route to success. They're greedy for the little things, often forgetting to see the bigger picture.

They usually have unsuccessful marriages because they are unable to hold back their words when they should, and they also struggle with issues of honesty.

口相

Crooked Mouth
歪斜口

A Crooked Mouth is defined by one where the lips obviously slant to one side. If the lips slant to the left, it indicates the person is likely to have problems with his or her father. If it slants to the right, the problem is with the mother.

People with a Crooked Mouth are hasty and rash, lacking proper goals and plans in life and blurting things out that they don't really mean!

They usually distort the facts, not so much because they want to lie, but because they are unable to present the plain facts without either adding to or subtracting from it. They are also the types who will hold grudges.

口相

The Flagged Mouth
令旗口

A Flagged Mouth is a mouth where the middle indentation on the upper lip, the two points which together form the shape of the letter 'M' (and also known as the 'flags') is sharp and well-defined.

This indicates a person who is extremely skillful in speech, and who is able to be powerfully persuasive with their words. They are able to communicate their thoughts with passion and articulation, and are never the ones who are at a loss for words!

These are the types of people whose words are able to touch another person deeply. Usually, they also possess good sales abilities and are quite influential and can hold others in their verbal spell.

口相

29

Smiling Mouth 上昇形口

A smiling mouth refers to, as the name suggests, a mouth where the corners are gently turned upwards, as if the person is constantly smiling. This is one of the most ideal mouth types to have – so if you have one, you have plenty of reason to smile!

A Smiling Mouth indicates a jovial, happy character for whom the glass is always half full. They will find it easy to achieve success due to their positive mindset.

They're always surrounded by good friends, and they will be a good friend in return – being the type of people who will always come running when you call, even if the call is at 3 am!

口相

Wrinkled Mouth 皺紋口

A wrinkled mouth is one that looks like crushed paper, with lines covering the entire lip area, as well as the area around the mouth. People with wrinkled mouths will generally endure poor and weakened health.

People with Wrinkled Mouths are also lonely and unsociable, who will lack for friends and have unsatisfactory relationships. They will find it hard to trust others, and as such will be isolated from even friends and family members.

They have a negative view on money in general, and tend to believe that it is the root of all evil. As such, they will find it difficult to become wealthy themselves.

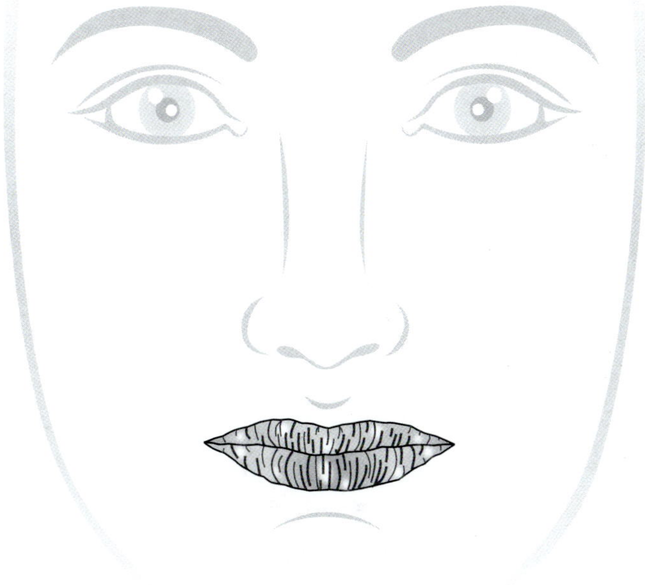

Wavering Mouth
口唇急荡

When someone is said to have a Wavering Mouth, that means the mouth is unable to close properly, leaving a gap of space that makes the teeth visible. Sometimes, the mouth continues to move or "waver" even after the last word has been uttered.

This means that the person has a very hurried, rash manner of being, and is easily influenced by others. This is exacerbated by their sense of naiveté and susceptibility.

Because of their hasty decisions, they're also constantly landing in hot water! That wouldn't be so bad if they had the wisdom to undo their own mistakes, but they rarely don't, preferring instead to follow the latest fad or trend instead of thinking for themselves.

口相

Lower Reserved Mouth 下反口

A person with a Lower Reserved Mouth usually possesses good stamina, with a strong sense of vitality. They are very charismatic when they speak, and will often achieve an elevated and influential position in society.

However, they lack a certain sentimental touch despite being compassionate and helpful. Their kindness is more of a hard-boiled kind, believing that one must sometimes be cruel to be kind, hence they are perceived as being unfeeling.

In their old age, their idealistic perception in life might paradoxically cause them to become stubborn, being fixated on certain ideals. They will become temperamental and often run into setbacks and obstacles.

口相

Revealing Mouth
掀露口

The Revealing Mouth refers to a mouth where the lower lip is perpetually open, revealing the lower teeth. This type of mouth denotes a person who is unable to get along with his or her father or father figure in life.

People with Revealing Mouths are usually mentally imbalanced, possessing extremes of emotions and opinions. They are constantly criticizing others for a variety of real or imagined faults, and get into a lot of arguments because of this.

They typically tend to lack a certain sense of self-control, and enjoy throwing out ultimatums to others as a form of gaining control. This is why they seldom have a lot of close friends.

口相

39

Unrevealed Teeth Mouth 口不見齒

A mouth with Unrevealed Teeth is one where the lips are able to close completely over the teeth while the face is relaxed. This is the type of person where what you see is what you get, no less and no more.

They are typically trustworthy people who treat others with honesty. Everything they do and say is sincere. They are not the types to boast and show off, as this is something they quite strongly dislike.

People with this type of mouth are good listeners, and even better at keeping secrets. If you need to keep something hush-hush, these are the people to whom you can safely reveal all without worrying about it spreading around town!

口相
41

The Drooling Mouth

夜糟糟

The Drooling Mouth is pretty much self-explanatory, but it doesn't necessarily have to denote actual drooling. It could also mean a mouth where the lips are constantly wet due to excess saliva.

Babies and elderly people drool, and it's considered normal. On elderly people, in fact, it denotes longevity. But on a regular person who is not a baby or a senior citizen, drooling is not a good sign.

It suggests possible health problems, especially where the bladder and reproductive organs are concerned. Drooling in a regular adult person could also indicate issues with blood circulation. It would be best to schedule an appointment with a doctor soon.

43

Upper Lip 'Biting' Lower Lip 偃蹇口

When a person is said to have an Upper Lip Biting Lower Lip mouth, it indicates that the lips are unable to close properly due to an imbalance in the thickness of the lips. The upper lip protrudes over the lower lip.

People with this type of mouth usually suffer from topsy-turvy emotions, and can be prone to extremes. They typically lack the wisdom needed to sift through their wildly-oscillating feelings.

They are prone to being show-offs, and enjoy being part of the popularity contest. They enjoy the materialistic, showy lifestyle and culture. Health-wise, they're not always in top form, and tend to suffer from issues with their digestive system and blood circulation.

口相

Lower Lip 'Biting' Upper Lip 下包上

When a mouth is said to be a Lower Lip Biting Upper Lip type, it generally indicates that the lower lip is more pronounced than the upper lip. It protrudes out to the point where it looks like it's 'biting into' the upper lip.

People with this type of mouth are quite selfish and self-centered, and have a serious case of 'Me-syndrome,' where everything ideally revolves around them! They can also be a tiny bit obsessive about keeping their surroundings clean and tidy.

Interestingly enough, they also have a very strong sexual drive. And because they consider themselves the most important creatures on the planet, they adore being pampered and love to enjoy the luxuries of life.

口相

Lines on Lower Lips
下唇有紋

People with Lines on Lower Lips have a very heavily-lined lower lip in contrast to the upper lip, and the rest of the mouth. Lines on the Lower Lips indicate a happy-go-lucky character who is able to endure hardships without much complaint.

They are usually genuinely nice people, although sometimes a bit naïve. However, they lack the gumption to criticise others, and if the lower lip is thicker than the upper lip, than they are a lot more self-conscious.

On the whole, they generally lack courage and often opt out of something for not having the nerve. They do not enjoy being put under the limelight and are much happier to remain in the background.

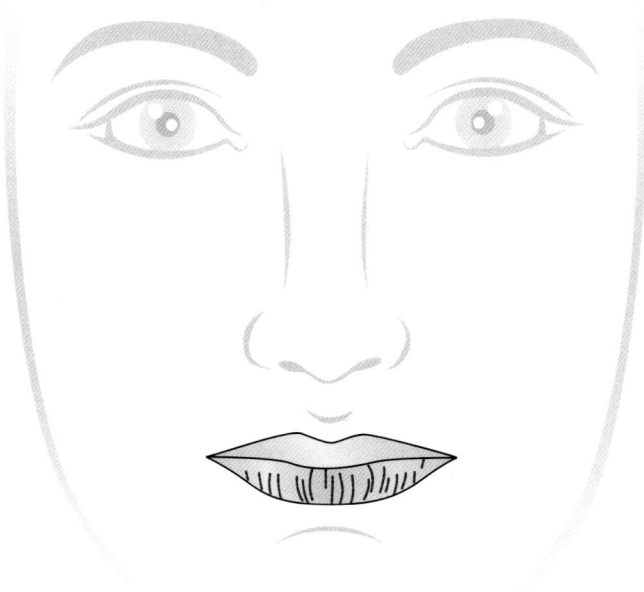

口相

Unbalanced Lips
歪嘴唇

When we talk about Unbalanced Lips, we mean a mouth where the one of the corners of the mouth slopes upward while the other slopes downward, giving the mouth a somewhat lopsided appearance.

A person with this mouth is usually stubborn and quick to anger, and a meddling personality who likes to interfere in others' affairs. They like to argue just for the sake of arguing, and are good at scolding and telling others off.

While they have verbal dexterity, when confronted by someone stronger or more powerful they usually fall silent. They like to fob off their tasks and duties to others. As a result, other people tend to want to avoid them!

口相

51

Protruding Lips 凸唇

Protruding Lips refers to a mouth where the lips jut out quite obviously, especially when seen in profile. People with this mouth are often hedonistic and materialistic, with a strong sexual appetite.

They also tend to be rash and gullible, because they don't pay attention to the details or the unsaid things. Quick-tempered, aggressive, and stubborn, they will rarely back down from a fight.

They also tend to be the ones sticking their feet in their mouths and telling others off before finding out the facts. As a result, they will have very few friends left in their old age and will often lead a lonely and isolated life.

口相

Sunken Lips 凹唇

Sunken Lips refer to a mouth that appears to sink inwards on a face, especially when seen from the profile. People with Sunken Lips often tend to be introverts who don't easily reveal their thoughts or feelings.

To others, they are a constant enigma. It's hard to know what's really going on in their minds without some artful prodding. They are also very remorseful and quick to feel regret.

They are prone to being self-contradictory, as they often want to speak up to their friends and acquaintances, and yet they don't for fear of offending others. Always wanting to weigh every option before committing to a decision, they tend to miss the boat on good opportunities.

口相

55

Solitary Life Lines
孤壽紋

A mouth that has Solitary Life Lines is a mouth that has two obvious and visible lines stretching and curving downward from the corners of the mouth. This mouth denotes a long life.

However, it's likely to be a hard life. People with Solitary Life Lines will always be working or kept busy even until their old age. They will also be constant worriers.

Loneliness is a key factor in their lives, and they will not have many friends with whom to share their problems. If they have children, they will not enjoy the company of their kids – or the children may not grow up to be successful.

口相

Unique Mouth Shapes

Blowing Fire Mouth
吹火口

The Blowing Fire Mouth is called as such because the mouth is unable to close properly, giving the person an appearance of someone about to blow on candles!

It's also sometimes known as Thunder Mouth 雷公嘴.

They usually talk without thinking, being prone to utter inane and silly things that can sometimes offend others. They're unwise and don't exercise much analytical thought, and thus easily hurt the feelings of others.

Because they're careless and lack self control, they aren't quite able to achieve much success in life. And because they tend to drive people away with their thoughtless comments, they're also likely to be lonely in their old age.

口相

Cherry Mouth
櫻桃口

A Cherry Mouth is defined as a mouth that has upward-sloping, rounded corners – with full, red lips that close perfectly over the teeth. Generally, the Cherry Mouth can be found on females more than males.

People with a Cherry Mouth are usually very intelligent and witty, with a diplomatic and tactful manner of speech. They are loveable by nature, and are able to attract people easily. They can manage and express their emotions well, and will always do their best in every situation.

On ladies with round, fleshy chins, a Cherry Mouth denotes someone who will take good care of her children and husband, and who will enjoy a life of domestic bliss and contentment.

口相

Lotus Leaf Mouth

荷葉邊口

A Lotus Leaf Mouth is a mouth that takes on the shape of a lotus leaf, with thin, dull-coloured lips that lack freshness and vitality. It is typically quite long, and curves downward.

People with Lotus Leaf Mouths can't walk past your table without passing a comment on something, and are always generous with their criticism and enthusiastic about gossip. Rest assured that if you make a mistake, they will only be too happy to remind you of it – over and over again!

Nothing is ever good enough for them, and as a result others will find them annoying. They will also find it hard to obtain peace of mind and be stress-free.

口相

Grained Mouth 熟粟口

A Grained Mouth appears when there are tiny, faint lines appearing all around, like little grains around the mouth. This is usually an indication of unfavourable family luck, as people with a Grained Mouth are likely to enjoy very little affinity with their family members.

A marked trait of people with Grained Mouths is their inability to appreciate good food. They wouldn't know a gourmet dish even if they bit into it!

Their character is sometimes like a closed book, and they don't share their thoughts easily. In fact, they are often quite solitary by nature and will rarely be the type who "spills the beans"! Due to their reticence, they will also suffer from a lonely old age.

口相

Satchel Mouth 口如拓囊

A Satchel Mouth is called as such because the mouth looks pursed and compact, somewhat like a tightened satchel or shoulder bag! A mouth like this points toward a lack of prosperity and happiness during a person's old age.

The Satchel Mouth also indicates that a person is not good at saving or accumulating money, and usually suffers from a lack of it. Being somewhat miserly and stingy, they are not likely to part with their money easily!

In general, people with Satchel Mouths also often lead lonely lives. They're not likely to blaze their own path, and are more likely to be followers than leaders

口相

Crescent Moon Mouth
仰月口

A Crescent Moon Mouth is similar to the Smiling Mouth, but in this case, the lower lip is wider and broader, giving the mouth the shape of a crescent moon. The Crescent Moon Mouth is also a bigger, wider, and longer than the Smiling Mouth.

Just like the Smiling Mouth personality, people with this type of mouth are loveable characters who always see the bright side of things and look for the silver lining in every cloud.

The Crescent Moon Mouth person is an epicurean and an appreciator of the finer things in life. They enjoy good food, fine wine, and all the delicious little luxuries of life! They're also powerfully articulate with words, and are very persuasive and influential.

口相

Bow-Shaped Mouth 궁구

The Bow-Shaped Mouth can be identified by an upper lip that is slightly longer than the lower lip, with both upper and lower lips being of similar thickness. The corners of the upper lip gently and subtly tilt upward.

People with this mouth are likely to be of a gentle and mild nature, sentimental souls who value intellectual ideals and knowledge over material acquisitions. They also value friendship highly, and enjoy making new friends at every opportunity.

You'll notice that people with Bow-Shaped Mouths love to be flattered, which might make it easier for you to become friends with them! But it's sincere flattery or praise that will win them over.

口相

Curved Bow Crescent Moon Mouth 彎弓仰月口

The Curved Bow Crescent Moon Mouth has the combined physical characteristics of both the Crescent Moon Mouth and the Bow-Shaped Mouth.

People with the Curved Bow Crescent Moon Mouth are extremely intelligent, and have superior orator skills. They know how to communicate well with others, and will typically tend to excel as politicians or in public office.

They will usually be good leaders, and people will naturally gravitate to them for guidance. They will also be the ones laughing all the way to the bank, as they know how to become wealthy and – most importantly – how to enjoy it and make the most of it!

口相

Swoosh Shape Mouth 乀型口

The person with a Swoosh Shape Mouth has good stamina coupled with a strong sense of endurance. He or she is usually very focused and driven at work, and usually as stubborn as an ox! The plus point is that people of this nature do not give up easily and are relentless in accomplishing their goals.

If you run into any problems, seek out the person with the Swoosh Shape Mouth, as this is the person who will help people out in times of need. They enjoy being in the middle of things, assisting others to settle their problems and concerns.

Being energetic, sporty, and action-oriented, their motto might quite suitably be "Just do it!"

口相
77

Sword Handle Mouth
劍鐔口

The Sword Handle Mouth has a square-like appearance with thick lips, resembling the protruding section in the sword where the handle and blade are connected.

People with Sword Handle Mouths are usually righteous, upright souls who always believe in the doing the easy thing – even if it's not the easiest thing. They will never take the morally-weak shortcut. They are forgiving in nature and are not the type to hold on to grudges and resentment.

They are very altruistic and selfless, and the key tenets that underlie their thoughts and actions are loyalty, friendship, and peace. As such, they are often the truest type of friend to have.

口相

Ocean Mouth 海口

When we say that someone has an Ocean Mouth, we mean that they have a very large mouth with well-defined borders, both on the upper and lower lips. It is a well marked-out mouth.

People with the Ocean Mouth are often very sincere and heartfelt with their words and deeds. They tend to be wise people whom others turn to for advice, and will have many friends and acquaintances all over the world.

It will be ideal for them to pursue careers in water-related industries such as transportation, travel, shipping, entertainment, and entertainment. People with an Ocean Mouth will also enjoy a very happy, productive, and contented latter part of life.

口相

81

Reverse Boat Mouth
覆船口

A Reverse Boat Mouth is a mouth that is perpetually turned downward, like a boat in reverse! People with this mouth usually endure difficult, desolate lives.

While young, they may have been abused or neglected, while their middle age is marked by feelings of unworthiness and dissatisfaction. Their old age is usually lonely and isolated.

As they largely have a pessimistic view of life, they are gloomy and forbidding, rarely tasting the pleasures life has to offer. They may be unusually stingy and calculative, expecting others to help without offering anything of their own in return. This is because they mostly feel like what they have to give is not of any value.

口相

Pearl in the Sea Mouth
嘴唇有珠

A Pearl in the Sea Mouth has a slight protuberance at the central tips of the lips. In Mian Xiang, the 'pearl' is also known as the Water Star. The Pearl in the Sea mouth is generally a good mouth for a lawyer to have!

This is because people with this type of mouth are gifted with the ability to debate and argue convincingly. They have a strong desire to win any argument, and will present their case in a persuasive, forceful, and articulate manner as to beat down any opponent!

In this case, it is a good mouth for a lawyer to have. They will be winning their cases with ease!

85

Island in the Sea Mouth
唇上有痣

An Island in the Sea Mouth is one where there is a mole visible on the lips. This is not a very good mouth to have, as it denotes problems in the digestive system for people with an Island in the Sea Mouth.

Possible health problems related to the digestive system can include intestinal problems, or the occurrence of kidney stones.

People with Island in the Sea Mouth are also always susceptible to suffering from food poisoning, and as such need to extra cautious about the things they eat. They need to be additionally invested in watching their dietary habits when compared to other people.

口相

87

Animal Shape Mouths

Monkey Mouth 猴口

When we say a person has a Monkey Mouth, it means that the person has a very large, wide mouth with equally wide lips. Their philtrum (the indented space between the nose and the lips) is also long and deep.

A Monkey Mouth denotes a good and strong family background, and it indicates that the person is likely to enjoy happy coincidences and events for the most part of his or her life.

These are the kind of people who will never lack for anything, and will have enough to eat and wear throughout all their lives. In general, the Monkey Mouth suggests abundance in life and longevity.

口相

Snake Mouth 蛇口

A Snake Mouth is one where the mouth protrudes slightly, giving the person the appearance of not having any lips. A unique attribute of people with Snake Mouths is that their tongue always juts out to moisten their lips.

People with Snake Mouths are not to be easily trusted at all, as they have a suspicious nature that is reflected in their attitude. They expect the worst from others and treat others badly, and as such they can be counted on to take advantage of people.

Due to their sly and cunning nature, they have a very strong tendency to lie and cheat their way into or out of a situation.

口相

Cow Mouth 牛口

People with Cow Mouths are generally very calm, steady, and stable, and will not be blown about by every wind. They are usually very conservative and trustworthy, and will be the kind you can rely on for every emergency.

They believe in hard work paving the path to true and genuine success, and as such will not be the ones to try to take a quick or sneaky shortcut. They will usually just hunker down and perform the work that is expected of them.

As befitting the animal from which the name is derived, people with Cow Mouths are of a gentle, peaceable nature. They don't enjoy or thrive on conflicts, and will always try to work for peace.

口相

95

Pigeon Mouth 鸽子口

A Pigeon Mouth refers to a very small mouth with pointy tips and edges. It is accompanied by equally small, round eyes. People with Pigeon Mouths are usually afraid of most things in life!

They worry too much and suffer from excess anxiety, mainly because they are constantly intimidated by the big, bad events and occurrences in the world. These are type of people who would rather be safe and secure than take any big risks.

In addition, they're constant complainers and always find a lack in everything. While they're afraid to be shortchanged in life, they also complain about being shortchanged, and as a result are likely to be shortchanged!

口
相

97

Dragon Mouth 龍口

A Dragon Mouth refers to a mouth where the upper and lower lips are both long, and equally thick and fleshy. The mouth corners are sharp, and it appears to rise or tilt upward.

People with Dragon Mouths are usually very adaptive, with quick reflexes and fast reactions. They are the kind who think on their feet and already have an answer or solution for you before you're even finished with your question!

They have a strong sense of determination and perseverance, and possess fantastic networking skills. They can easily form connection with others. As a result, more often than not, they will be able to derive opportunities for success and excellence through these connections.

口相

99

Horse Mouth 馬口

A person is said to have a Horse Mouth when he or she possesses a large mouth with big, uneven, and protruding teeth. In some cases, there may be a slight case of drooling involved.

There's a reason why everyone always hears it from the Horse's Mouth – because people with this type of mouth are unable to keep secrets! They talk a lot, and they talk loudly – on top of having a fondness for gossip and rumours.

They typically lack elegance and sophistication in their speech, and tend to shoot off their mouth without thinking. Because of this, they rarely rise to the upper echelons of society.

口相

101

Carp Mouth 鯽魚口

When we say Carp Mouth, we mean a mouth that is somewhat small, with the edges of the mouth downturned. The lips also appear to be perpetually pursed and puckered.

People who possess a Carp Mouth are critical of others, but blind to their own faults. They are constantly on a mission to compare everything to everything else! Arguments are a source of amusement to them, but only if they win each one.

The Carp Mouthed person will also have difficulties holding down a stable job, and will run into problems interacting with colleagues. Also, their old age will be largely unstable and full of obstacles, due to constant moving about and a lack of a regular income.

口相

Fish Head Mouth
鮎魚口

A Fish Head Mouth is defined as a big mouth with thin lips. The mouth corners turn downwards. Sometimes, there is a white-tinged substance found at the edges of the mouth, occasionally appearing like bubbles.

People with Fish Mouths are always somehow drawn into or involved in other people's drama. Mainly, this is because of their helpful nature – but sometimes this backfires on them and they find themselves involved in sticky messes that have nothing to do with them!

While they're motivated by a kind and compassionate nature, they are also often unaccountably curious – some may even say nosy! However, they rarely ever want to satiate their inquisitiveness for malicious or self-serving purposes.

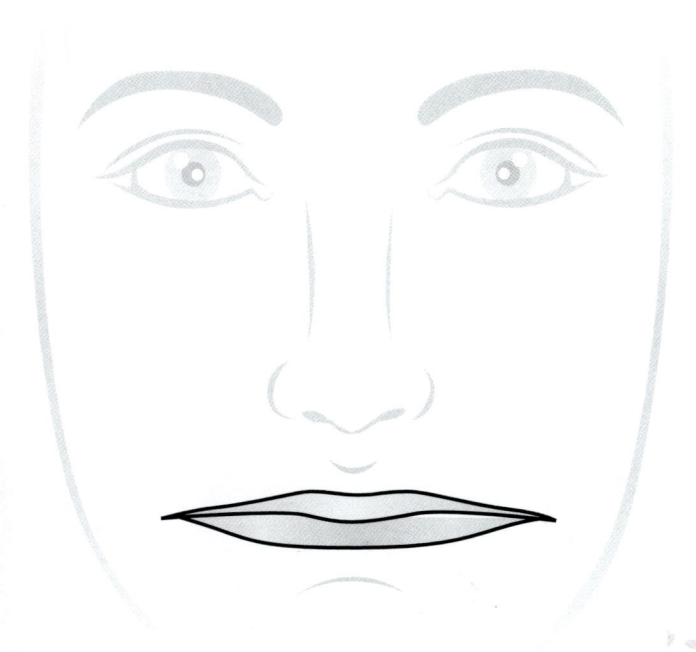

口相

Bird Beak Mouth

鳥喙口

A Bird Beak Mouth is one that protrudes out like the beak of a bird, especially when seen in profile. It reveals a clever character that is good at making thorough plans, yet is ruthless and unmerciful.

They are typically known for being poker faces, and do not reveal their feelings easily. Whether they're elated or morose, it's all kept within – one usually has a hard time guessing their feelings.

While they are good friends to have in tough times, they can't maintain long-term partnerships, because when things are going well they always want more of the share. When someone is no longer of use to them, they tend to cut them out of their lives.

口相

Rat Mouth 鼠口

To identify a Rat Mouth, look for a mouth that is thin, small, and sharp in appearance. Usually, a Rat Mouth is accompanied by an equally small-sounding, soft voice.

They tend to nibble when eating, consuming small portions of food very swiftly. They usually have the appearance of being scared all the time. A Rat Mouthed person is typically quite petty, with a focus on all things shallow and superficial.

Rat Mouths are greedy, and try to constantly take advantage of others. At the same time, they simper and suck up to others to get ahead, and trade in rumours and gossip. They lack gratitude and will never be appropriately thankful for anything.

口相

Tiger Mouth 虎口

A Tiger Mouth's most defining characteristic is its largeness – a whole fist can fit inside! This is a special but rare feature, because it denotes an extraordinary, noble, and magnanimous personality that enjoys wide respect and esteem.

People with Tiger Mouths are usually very capable and talented, and have a strong sense of determination. They never waver in their decisions, and are always the one initiating action.

They have a solid and strong sense of leadership, and if the Tiger Mouth is combined with a large nose and fleshy chin, then this indicates a person who can achieve tremendous wealth.

口相

111

Goat Mouth 羊口

When a person is said to have a Goat Mouth, it means that they have a mouth that is long and inadequate-looking. The mouth will have no borders and will curve downward at the corners. Males with Goat Mouths will not have a moustache.

People with Goat Mouths are bad at making decisions as a result of being over-analytical. Others might find them boring, and they stick to their comfort zone and want only routines in life. As a result, they rarely enjoy happiness.

They will work hard and put in a lot of effort, but they rarely get to taste success in life. This is mainly due to their lack of ambition.

口相

Pig Mouth 豬口

People with Pig Mouths have upper lips that are distinctively longer than the lower lips, with the corners of the lips pointing downward. They also have sharp and uneven teeth.

People with Pig Mouths are very cautious and guarded, but this is because they are cunning and always have a hidden agenda. As such, they attribute motives to others due to their own manipulative nature.

Their most defining characteristic is doing things halfway. They switch jobs fairly frequently, and are rarely faithful in relationships. They also have trouble saving money. In general, they have trouble being consistent about the important things in life! People with Pig Mouths have characters that often seem crude and unrefined.

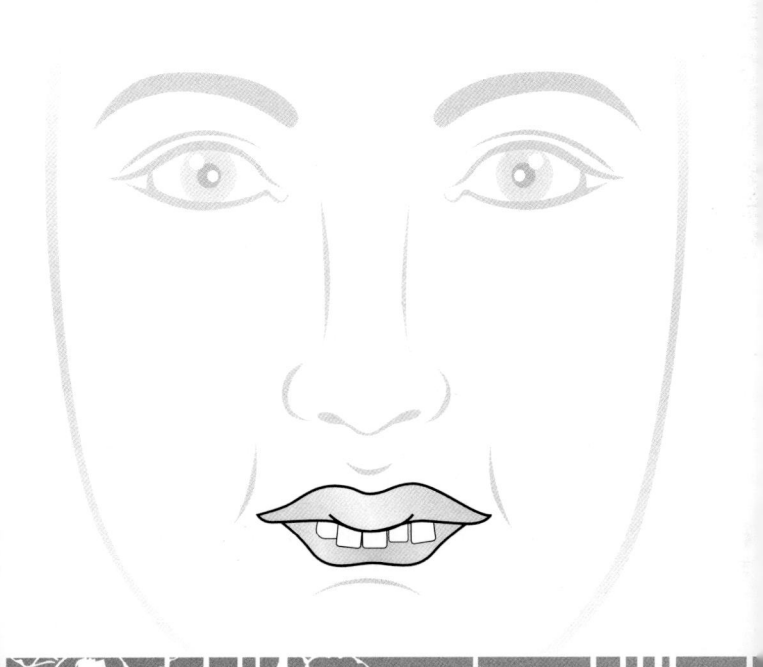

口相

About Joey Yap

Joey Yap is the Founder and Master Trainer of the Mastery Academy of Chinese Metaphysics, a global organization devoted to the teaching of Feng Shui, BaZi, Mian Xiang and other Chinese Metaphysics subjects. He is also the Chief Consultant of Yap Global Consulting, an international consulting firm specialising in Feng Shui and Chinese Astrology services and audits.

He is the bestselling author of over 25 books, including *Stories and Lessons on Feng Shui*, *BaZi – The Destiny Code*, *Mian Xiang – Discover Face Reading*, *Feng Shui for Homebuyers Series*, and *Pure Feng Shui*, which was released by an international publisher.

He is also the producer of the first comprehensive reference source of Chinese Metaphysics, **The Chinese Metaphysics Compendium**, a compilation of all the essential formulas and applications known and practiced in Chinese Metaphysics today. He has since produced various other reference books and workbooks to aid students in their study and practice of Chinese Metaphysics subjects.

An avid proponent of technology being the way forward in disseminating knowledge of Chinese Metaphysics, Joey has developed, among others, the **BaZi Ming Pan 2.0 Software** and the **Xuan Kong Flying Stars Feng Shui Software**. This passion for fusing the best of modern technology with the best of classical studies lead him to create one of the pioneer online schools for Chinese Metaphysics education, the Mastery Academy E-Learning Centre (www.maelearning.com).

In addition to being a regular guest on various international radio and TV shows, Joey has also written columns for leading newspapers, as well as having contributed articles for various international magazines and publications. He has been featured in many popular publications and media including *Time International*, *Forbes International*, the *International Herald Tribune*, and Bloomberg TV, and was selected as one of Malaysia Tatler's 'Most Influential People in Malaysia' in 2008.

A naturally engaging speaker, Joey has presented to clients like Citibank, HSBC, IBM, Microsoft, Sime Darby, Bloomberg, HP, Samsung, Mah Sing, Nokia, Dijaya, and Standard Chartered.

Joey has also hosted his own TV series, *Discovering Feng Shui with Joey Yap*, and appeared on Malaysia's Astro TV network's *Walking the Dragons with Joey Yap*.

Joey's updates can be followed via Twitter at **www.twitter.com/joeyyap**. A full list of recent events and updates, and more information, can be found at **www.joeyyap.com** and **www.masteryacademy.com**

EDUCATION
The Mastery Academy of Chinese Metaphysics:
the first choice for practitioners and aspiring students of the art and science of Chinese Classical Feng Shui and Astrology.

For thousands of years, Eastern knowledge has been passed from one generation to another through the system of discipleship. A venerated master would accept suitable individuals at a young age as his disciples, and informally through the years, pass on his knowledge and skills to them. His disciples in turn, would take on their own disciples, as a means to perpetuate knowledge or skills.

This system served the purpose of restricting the transfer of knowledge to only worthy honourable individuals and ensuring that outsiders or Westerners would not have access to thousands of years of Eastern knowledge, learning and research.

However, the disciple system has also resulted in Chinese Metaphysics and Classical Studies lacking systematic teaching methods. Knowledge garnered over the years has not been accumulated in a concise, systematic manner, but scattered amongst practitioners, each practicing his/her knowledge, art and science, in isolation.

The disciple system, out of place in today's modern world, endangers the advancement of these classical fields that continue to have great relevance and application today.

At the Mastery Academy of Chinese Metaphysics, our Mission is to bring Eastern Classical knowledge in the fields of metaphysics, Feng Shui and Astrology sciences and the arts to the world. These Classical teachings and knowledge, previously shrouded in secrecy and passed on only through the discipleship system, are adapted into structured learning, which can easily be understood, learnt and mastered. Through modern learning methods, these renowned ancient arts, sciences and practices can be perpetuated while facilitating more extensive application and understanding of these classical subjects.

The Mastery Academy espouses an educational philosophy that draws from the best of the East and West. It is the world's premier educational institution for the study of Chinese Metaphysics Studies offering a wide range and variety of courses, ensuring that students have the opportunity to pursue their preferred field of study and enabling existing practitioners and professionals to gain cross-disciplinary knowledge that complements their current field of practice.

Courses at the Mastery Academy have been carefully designed to ensure a comprehensive yet compact syllabus. The modular nature of the courses enables students to immediately begin to put their knowledge into practice while pursuing continued study of their field and complementary fields. Students thus have the benefit of developing and gaining practical experience in tandem with the expansion and advancement of their theoretical knowledge.

Students can also choose from a variety of study options, from a distance learning program, the Homestudy Series, that enables study at one's own pace or intensive foundation courses and compact lecture-based courses, held in various cities around the world by Joey Yap or our licensed instructors. The Mastery Academy's faculty and make-up is international in nature, thus ensuring that prospective students can attend courses at destinations nearest to their country of origin or with a licensed Mastery Academy instructor in their home country.

The Mastery Academy provides 24x7 support to students through its Online Community, with a variety of tools, documents, forums and e-learning materials to help students stay at the forefront of research in their fields and gain invaluable assistance from peers and mentoring from their instructors.

MASTERY ACADEMY
OF CHINESE METAPHYSICS

www.masteryacademy.com

MALAYSIA
19-3, The Boulevard, Mid Valley City, 59200 Kuala Lumpur, Malaysia
Tel : +603-2284 8080   Fax : +603-2284 1218   Email : info@masteryacademy.com

SINGAPORE
14, Robinson Road # 13-00, Far East Finance Building, Singapore 048545
Tel : +65-6494 9147   Email : singapore@masteryacademy.com

Australia, Austria, Canada, China, Croatia, Cyprus, Czech Republic, Denmark, France, Germany, Greece, Hungary, India, Italy, Kazakhstan, Malaysia, Netherlands (Holland), New Zealand, Philippines, Poland, Russian Federation, Singapore, Slovenia, South Africa, Switzerland, Turkey, U.S.A., Ukraine, United Kingdom

Mastery Academy around the world

Canada
United States
United Kingdom
Denmark
Netherlands
France
Switzerland
Czech Republic
Austria
Germany
Italy
Cyprus
Poland
Slovenia
Hungary
Croatia
Greece
Russian Federation
Ukraine
Turkey
Kazakhstan
China
India
South Africa
Philippines
Kuala Lumpur
Malaysia
Singapore
Australia
New Zealand

YAP GLOBAL CONSULTING

Joey Yap & Yap Global Consulting

Headed by Joey Yap, Yap Global Consulting (YGC) is a leading international consulting firm specializing in Feng Shui, Mian Xiang (Face Reading) and BaZi (Destiny Analysis) consulting services worldwide. Joey - an internationally renowned Master Trainer, Consultant, Speaker and best-selling Author - has dedicated his life to the art and science of Chinese Metaphysics.

YGC has its main offices in Kuala Lumpur and Australia, and draws upon its diverse reservoir of strength from a group of dedicated and experienced consultants based in more than 30 countries, worldwide.

As the pioneer in blending established, classical Chinese Metaphysics techniques with the latest approach in consultation practices, YGC has built its reputation on the principles of professionalism and only the highest standards of service. This allows us to retain the cutting edge in delivering Feng Shui and Destiny consultation services to both corporate and personal clients, in a simple and direct manner, without compromising on quality.

Across Industries: Our Portfolio of Clients

Our diverse portfolio of both corporate and individual clients from all around the world bears testimony to our experience and capabilities.

Virtually every industry imaginable has benefited from our services - ranging from academic and financial institutions, real-estate developers and multinational corporations, to those in the leisure and tourism industry. Our services are also engaged by professionals, prominent business personalities, celebrities, high-profile politicians and people from all walks of life.

YAP GLOBAL CONSULTING

Name (Mr./Mrs./Ms.):

Contact Details

Tel: _____ Fax: _____

Mobile: _____

E-mail: _____

What Type of Consultation Are You Interested In?
☐ Feng Shui ☐ BaZi ☐ Date Selection ☐ Yi Jing

Please tick if applicable:
☐ Are you a Property Developer looking to engage Yap Global Consulting?

☐ Are you a Property Investor looking for tailor-made packages to suit your investment requirements?

Please attach your name card here.

Thank you for completing this form.
Please fax it back to us at:

Singapore
Tel : +65-6494 9147

Malaysia & the rest of the world
Fax: +603-2284 2213
Tel : +603-2284 1213

---

www.joeyyap.com

www.joeyyap.com

Feng Shui Consultations

For Residential Properties
- Initial Land/Property Assessment
- Residential Feng Shui Consultations
- Residential Land Selection
- End-to-End Residential Consultation

For Commercial Properties
- Initial Land/Property Assessment
- Commercial Feng Shui Consultations
- Commercial Land Selection
- End-to-End Commercial Consultation

For Property Developers
- End-to-End Consultation
- Post-Consultation Advisory Services
- Panel Feng Shui Consultant

For Property Investors
- Your Personal Feng Shui Consultant
- Tailor-Made Packages

For Memorial Parks & Burial Sites
- Yin House Feng Shui

BaZi Consultations

Personal Destiny Analysis
- Personal Destiny Analysis for Individuals
- Children's BaZi Analysis
- Family BaZi Analysis

Strategic Analysis for Corporate Organizations
- Corporate BaZi Consultations
- BaZi Analysis for Human Resource Management

Entrepreneurs & Business Owners
- BaZi Analysis for Entrepreneurs

Career Pursuits
- BaZi Career Analysis

Relationships
- Marriage and Compatibility Analysis
- Partnership Analysis

For Everyone
- Annual BaZi Forecast
- Your Personal BaZi Coach

Date Selection Consultations

- **Marriage Date Selection**
- **Caesarean Birth Date Selection**
- **House-Moving Date Selection**
- **Renovation & Groundbreaking Dates**
- **Signing of Contracts**
- **Official Openings**
- **Product Launches**

Yi Jing Assessment

A Time-Tested, Accurate Science

- With a history predating 4 millennia, the Yi Jing - or Classic of Change - is one of the oldest Chinese texts surviving today. Its purpose as an oracle, in predicting the outcome of things, is based on the variables of Time, Space and Specific Events.

- A Yi Jing Assessment provides specific answers to any specific questions you may have about a specific event or endeavor. This is something that a Destiny Analysis would not be able to give you.

Basically, what a Yi Jing Assessment does is focus on only ONE aspect or item at a particular point in your life, and give you a calculated prediction of the details that will follow suit, if you undertake a particular action. It gives you an insight into a situation, and what course of action to take in order to arrive at a satisfactory outcome at the end of the day.

Please Contact YGC for a personalized Yi Jing Assessment!

Tel: +603-2284 1213   Email: consultation@joeyyap.com

www.joeyyap.com

INVITING US TO YOUR CORPORATE EVENTS

Many reputable organizations and institutions have worked closely with YGC to build a synergistic business relationship by engaging our team of consultants, led by Joey Yap, as speakers at their corporate events. Our seminars and short talks are always packed with audiences consisting of clients and associates of multinational and public-listed companies as well as key stakeholders of financial institutions.

We tailor our seminars and talks to suit the anticipated or pertinent group of audience. Be it a department, subsidiary, your clients or even the entire corporation, we aim to fit your requirements in delivering the intended message(s).

Tel: +603-2284 1213   Email: consultation@joeyyap.com

Educational Tools & Software

Xuan Kong Flying Stars Feng Shui Software
The Essential Application for Enthusiasts and Professionals

Highlights of the software include:
- Natal Flying Stars
- Monthly Flying Stars
- 81 Flying Stars Combinations
- Dual-View Format
- Annual Flying Stars
- Flying Stars Integration
- 24 Mountains

All charts will be are printable and configurable, and can be saved for future editing. Also, you'll be able to export your charts into most image file formats like jpeg, bmp, and gif.

Mini Feng Shui Compass

The Mini Feng Shui Compass is a self-aligning compass that is not only light at 100gms but also built sturdily to ensure it will be convenient to use anywhere. The rings on the Mini Feng Shui Compass are bi-lingual and incorporate the 24 Mountain Rings that is used in your traditional Luo Pan.

BaZi Ming Pan Software Version 2.0
Professional Four Pillars Calculator for Destiny Analysis

The BaZi Ming Pan Version 2.0 Professional Four Pillars Calculator for Destiny Analysis is the most technically advanced software of its kind in the world today. It allows even those without any knowledge of BaZi to generate their own BaZi Charts, and provides virtually every detail required to undertake a comprehensive Destiny Analysis.

Joey Yap Feng Shui Template Set

The Set comprises 3 basic templates: The Basic Feng Shui Template, 8 Mansions Feng Shui Template, and the Flying Stars Feng Shui Template.

Main Features:
- Easy-to-use, simple, and straightforward
- Small and portable; each template measuring only 5" x 5"
- Additional 8 Mansions and Flying Stars Reference Rings
- Handy companion booklet with usage tips and examples

Feng Shui for Homebuyers DVD Series

In these DVDs, Joey will guide you on how to customise your home to maximise the Feng Shui potential of your property and gain the full benefit of improving your health, wealth and love life using the 9 Palace Grid. He will show you how to go about applying the classical applications of the Life Gua and House Gua techniques to get attuned to your Sheng Qi (positive energies).

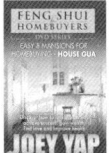

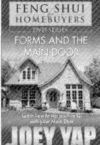

Accelerate Your Face Reading Skills With Joey Yap's Face Reading Revealed DVD Series

In these highly entertaining DVDs, Joey will help you answer all these questions and more. You will be able to ascertain the underlying meaning of moles, birthmarks or even the type of your hair in Face Reading. Joey will also reveal the guidelines to help you foster better and stronger relationships with your loved ones through Mian Xiang.

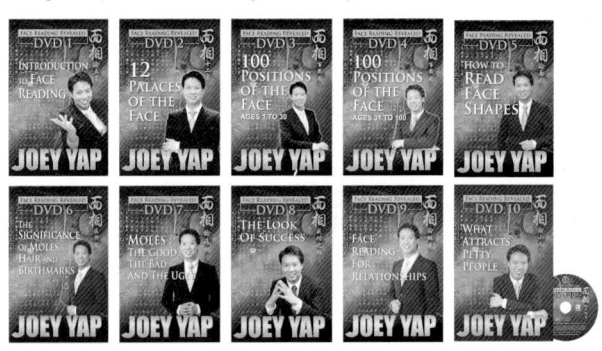

Discover Feng Shui with Joey Yap (TV Series) - Set of 4 DVDS

Informative and entertaining, classical Feng Shui comes alive in *Discover Feng Shui with Joey Yap!*

Own the series that national channel 8TV did a re-run of in 2005, today!

Book: Feng Shui for Homebuyers Series

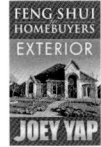

Feng Shui For Homebuyers - Exterior
(English & Chinese versions)

Feng Shui for Homebuyers - Interior

Feng Shui for Apartment Buyers - Home Owners

Book: Stories and Lessons on Feng Shui Series

Stories and Lessons on Feng Shui
(English & Chinese versions)

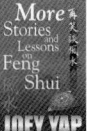

More Stories and Lessons on Feng Shui

Even More Stories and Lessons on Feng Shui

Book: BaZi - The Destiny Code Series

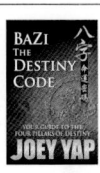

BaZi - The Destiny Code
(English & Chinese versions)

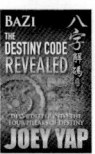

BaZi - The Destiny Code Revealed

Continue Your Journey with Joey Yap's Books

Walking the Dragons

Your Aquarium Here

The Art of Date Selection: Personal Date Selection

Mian Xiang - Discover Face Reading
(English & Chinese versions)

The Ten Thousand Year Calendar

Xuan Kong: Flying Stars Feng Shui

Elevate Your Feng Shui Skills With Joey Yap's Home Study Course And Educational DVDs

Xuan Kong Vol.1
An Advanced Feng Shui Home Study Course

Feng Shui for Period 8 - (DVD)

Xuan Kong Flying Stars Beginners Workshop - (DVD)

BaZi Four Pillars of Destiny Beginners Workshop - (DVD)

Interested in learning MORE about Feng Shui? Advance Your Feng Shui Knowledge with the Mastery Academy Courses.

Feng Shui Mastery Series™
LIVE COURSES (MODULES ONE TO FOUR)

The Feng Shui Mastery Series comprises Feng Shui Mastery Modules 1, 2, 3, and 4. It is a program that introduces students to the theories, principles, analyses, and interpretations of classical Feng Shui. It is a thorough, comprehensive program that covers important theories from various classical Feng Shui systems including Ba Zhai, San Yuan, San He, and Xuan Kong.

BaZi Mastery Series™
LIVE COURSES (MODULES ONE TO FOUR)

The BaZi Mastery Series comprises BaZi Mastery Modules 1, 2, 3, and 4 which provides students with a thorough introduction to BaZi, along with an intensive understanding of BaZi principles and the requisite skills to practice it with accuracy and precision. Students who complete these modules will be well-prepared to perform readings and interpretations. Feng Shui practitioners will also benefit from having knowledge of BaZi, as it will complement and enhance their Feng Shui practice.

XUAN KONG MASTERY SERIES™
LIVE COURSES (MODULES ONE TO THREE)
* Advanced Courses For Master Practitioners

The Xuan Kong Mastery Series allows students to take their introductory steps into the captivating world of this potent and powerful science. While Classical Feng Shui is always about the study of Location and Direction, Xuan Kong factors in the concept of Time into the equation as well. This course that will expose students to the extremely advanced techniques and formulas based upon those that were used by the ancient masters, as derived from the classics. It paves the way for students to specialize in the intelligent and strategic allocation of Qi, allowing them to literally manipulate Qi to assist in their life endeavours.

Mian Xiang Mastery Series™
LIVE COURSES (MODULES ONE AND TWO)

As one of the time-tested Five Arts (Wu Xing) of Chinese Metaphysics, Mian Xiang falls under the study of the physiognomy of the features, contours, shapes and hues of the face. In Mian Xiang, however, a person's face is more than what he or she shows the world; it's also a virtual map of this person's potential and destiny in life.

The Mian Xiang Mastery Series comprises Module 1 and Module 2 to allow students to learn this ancient art in a thorough, detailed manner. Each module has a carefully-developed syllabus that allows students to get acquainted with the fundamentals of Mian Xiang before moving on to the more intricate theories and principles that will enable them to practice Mian Xiang with greater depth and complexity.

Yi Jing Mastery Series™
LIVE COURSES (MODULES ONE AND TWO)

'Yi' relates to change. Indeed, flux - or continuous change - is the key concept of the Yi Jing. Change is the only constant in life, and there is no exception to this rule. Evolution, transformation, alteration - call it by any other name, its effects are still far-reaching and encompasses every law - natural or manmade - known to our universe.

The Yi Jing Mastery Series provides an introductory look into the basics and fundamentals of Yi Jing thought and theory. As the Yi Jing functioned as an ancient Chinese oracle thousands of years ago, this Module will explore Yi Jing as a science of divination and probe the ways in which the concept of 'change' plays a big part in Yi Jing. Together both modules aim to give casual and serious Yi Jing enthusiasts a serious insight into one of the most important philosophical treatises in ancient Chinese thought.

Ze Ri Mastery Series™
LIVE COURSES (MODULES ONE AND TWO)

The ZeRi Mastery Series, or Date Selection, comprise two modules: ZeRi Mastery Series Module 1 and ZeRi Mastery Series Module 2. This program provides students with a thorough introduction to the art of Date Selection both for Personal and Feng Shui purposes. Both modules provide a fundamental grounding in all the rudimentary basics and allow you to move from the more straightforward techniques in Module 1 to the more sophisticated methods of Xuan Kong Da Gua in Module 2 with ease and confidence.

Feng Shui for Life

Feng Shui for life is a 5-day course designed for the Feng Shui beginner to learn how to apply practical Feng Shui in day-to-day living. It is a culmination of powerful tools and techniques that allows you to gain quick proficiency in Classical Feng Shui.

Mastery Academy courses are conducted around the world. Find out when will Joey Yap be in your area by visiting **www.masteryacademy.com** or call our office at **+603-2284 8080**.